The Rules of Being Highly Skillful

30 Minutes Read

Deepak Gupta

Published by Inspirational Publishing, 2022.

Table of Contents

1. Title Page 1

2. Copyright © Deepak Gupta 2022 3

4. The Mind Emptiness: Why Skills are Significant! 4

5. You Don't Want What You Want: Prologue 7

6. Chapter 1: The Game of Memories: Mind Attention and Consciousness 10

7. Chapter 2: Good and Terrible Mistakes: The Compounding Effect 12

8. Chapter 3: The Slow Progress of Skills: Help Yourself . 14

9. Chapter 4: Fail the Tough Skills: How to Accept Any Tasks 16

10. Chapter 5: Visionary and Exciting Skills: Recognise What Everyone Else is Missing 18

11. Chapter 6: The Disturbing Elements in Your Work: Control them immediately 20

12. Chapter 7: Wander & Wonder: Replicate this! 23

13. Chapter 8: Eliminate, Essential, Execute 25

14. Chapter 9: Hit the Hard-Loved & Tough Skill: Strategy to Reduce Competition 28

15. Chapter 10: Active vs Passive Income: Are Both Significant? 30

16. Chapter 11: Introduce New Skills: The Loop of Solving Problems 32

17. Chapter 12: Skills Building on Internet: Opportunity But! 34

18. Chapter 13: What Hinders Our Skills Development: The Fear Factor Barrier 36

19. Chapter 14: The Significance of Dissatisfaction 37

20. Chapter 15: The Impossibility of Skills: Tough Skills in Life 38

21. Chapter 16: The Everyday Routine in Building Skills: Vital Rules for Implementation 40

22. Chapter 17: Complex Problems, Tough Procedure, & Simple Outcome: The Stages in Skill Development! 43

23. Chapter 18: One Day; One Task: The Mind Hack......45

24. Chapter 19: Brainstorming Skills: Never Get Bored with Them! 47

25. Chapter 20: The Core of Discipline: The Master Key.49

26. Chapter 21: Make Subconscious Skills Conscious: Repeat the Mind Exercise 51

27. Chapter 22: The Gist of Exercising & Implementation of Rules 53

28. About the Author 56

THE

RULES
OF BEING
HIGHLY
SKILLFUL

DEEPAK GUPTA

Copyright © Deepak Gupta 2022

The Mind Emptiness

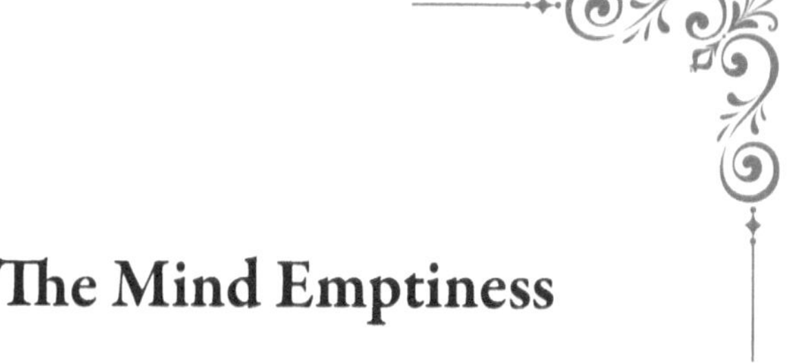

Why Skills are Significant!

It is necessary to work, if not from inclination, at least from despair. Everything considered, work is less boring than amusing oneself. - Charles Baudelaire.

Our human world is teeming with various baits and these baits hinder our ways to achieve what we genuinely want but also, we can't ignore these temptations because these baits express a fruitful and attentive recognition in society, like if we ignore money, people will call us fools. Most people compare money with progress and that's why people first go for money rather than to perform what can make their life good in the long run. These baits create the gulf to present an ordinary classification as a rich & poor sympathy of this world. Money, a lot of money, deep attraction, reputed work, extraordinary form of thinking, and a luxury life; these baits are always seen as a sign of success, where the people who try to get satisfied with what they possess, seen as the people who don't try to become best, even when they are satisfied with what they have. Work isn't what most people perform, but work is what, when they are immensely interested to adapt and accept it for a lifetime without losing enthusiasm in any situation of life. Many genius classic people died in poverty while loving and carrying out their work like an art, but became popular after people had gotten amused from their work.

Choosing honest work is tough these days because most people, families and friends expect a reputed and money-making work and yes, money fascinate us all in short and long run because it can get us what work solely can't but remember, without a deep work, money can become the short-term motivation and things may become messy in long run. Consequently, choosing the right work is significant to live your life happily, more significantly, in constant peace.

The world isn't working with a few people. Each and every person is working, even the animals, & that's how the world remains balanced. The world isn't run by money or highly reputed people, but with the balance of everything. God has chosen us for the work we genuinely like to do for a robust life.

The emptiness in today's generation represents the expectations of something best out of every ordinary. Choosing wrong work can disturb anyone, even if someone earns a lot of money with it. Our minds need something innovative and creative to refresh us with enthusiasm & joy. Skills in anyone's work retain some power to make people feel great and produce a sense of satisfaction after every petty accomplishment. If someone doesn't admire the work, then he will not like its accomplishment. *The skills can encourage you to find a life purpose, a passive source of income, to acquire freedom of time; let you enjoy life while approaching new people and experiences, create a great*

& fast rollercoaster to enjoy sight and develop enthusiasm every moment to refill the juice of life.

Skillful people don't win every day, but they win every moment for the rest of their lives. Make yourself a deserving person. When you feel like you are worthy to win, you will win, till then work like hell because in hell, even we never sleep.

You Don't Want
What You Want:
Prologue

5 years back, I approached a casual stranger in a metro. While talking I got to know, he was extremely gloomy with his routine life. His tough stressful bank job was sucking time fast; even earlier he wanted that job. He was tense and worried that he wasn't enjoying life like he always wanted. His soul was in agony, and he wanted to escape that job. I was surprised to find him stressed and unhappy because he had a decent job, security and handsome money to enjoy a great lifestyle. Regardless, I talked to him with less interest. That time I was doing my post-graduation from Delhi School of Economics and I also had the desire to get a job and make my life secure like youth wants. For me, it was a disgrace to appreciate his decision to resign from the job. I was entirely displeased with his opinion. Then, after a few weeks, I met my friend who was unhappy with his business. He was dealing with his father's business, but actually he wanted to do the job. Strange! There's a reason I'm describing these bizarre incidents. I was also curious & confused to recognize why people aren't satisfied, even though they have everything; money, decent work, and a quality standard of living. Are these things

not enough to lead a happy life? ***People don't want the enjoyment of a destination but to enjoy the process of achieving it. It's not about any job or business, but about the nature of the work they wanted.*** Every process leads to a destination, but after every destination, a process should start to give our life a supreme direction ahead. Apart from earning money, people desire a lot of activities and that's the secret ingredient to enjoying life. *Money is just money. Money has no satisfaction, but if we earn money with what we love, satisfaction in money arises.* We can almost achieve anything but can't enjoy everything equally and consistently.

I'm writing this book to make our life and money a deep sense of satisfaction. We can overlook the undesired effects and can be delighted after, but we can't ignore what we desire consciously and subconsciously. ***Life has no meaning with money only, but with the combination of skills and money, so that we can enjoy money as a secondary element and humanity can still prevail in this world.***

Skills, every time I listen to this word, I remember a sentence; good, peaceful, happy and joyful life. Anything that aids us to learn about our life and environment with optimum efforts and more enjoyment, can sum up the meaning of skills. Remember, skills aren't only good; they can be destructive & extremely bad. Skills can make our life brilliant or may be hell. Everything comes with advantages and disadvantages, both. Most people feel like they can acquire a skill in a few days, but it's not practically possible. Anything we don't enjoy and still become expert in it, can't enhance the skills because if you aren't enjoying it, you can't think positively about it and can't make improvements in it.

Skill isn't a plane surface. It comes after a series of stairs. Crush the paper and throw it in the distant bin. Alright, you can do that. You can do it once, twice, but not every time. Skills should only have room for improvement but not for degradation. When we undertake a particular task for one time only, it may be luck or mistake; but doing it more than once, like twice or thrice out of the total, can make it a series of habits. Yes, we can develop habits and they can be forgotten if we don't perform them regularly. When we try to do them again and again, we can include them in our daily practice. ***Practice doesn't make perfect if you're not interested in that.*** Practice with improvement makes skills. When you attain the ability to throw crushed paper into the bin every time you try, you will get the skills. And remember, whatever you learn, you also develop the capabilities to improve it. Capabilities aren't always there when we try to improve but develop with our problems. Skills that we don't upgrade, become useless after a time.

Money without family is useless, and family without money is also useless. In the first place, we need to understand what skills we undoubtedly have; then there are systematic procedures and methods to stand out uniquely in this world. Unique skills are always appreciated. The Rules of Being Highly Skillful isn't the book but the rollercoaster where you will read what I have been learning since my childhood. You are learning even when you don't pay attention, but when you understand and make it conscious in life, skills start to be born within us.

Chapter 1

The Game of Memories: Mind Attention and Consciousness

Do not remember anything, and you will be happy, and as well as you will learn nothing.

Our mind is simple and complex at the same time. Put differently, it can think as simple as it can and as difficult and tangled as we want. Mind doesn't control our body, but our mind and body control each other. They work like a jumping frog and in that, memories play a vital role in deciding our life skills. Skills are something like passion, and passion needs dedication and consciousness to every detail of our life. Whatever we undertake, we should be entirely conscious of knowing what we really like, so that we can make it in the long run. These kinds of habits aid us to perceive what we passionately love. There are seven kinds of memories that play a role in our lives. You know, the same person can control emotions, and the same person can get uncontrollable sometimes. It depends on how much consciousness we give to events. We have two types of significant memories; one is short, and the other is long. Short memories remain for 20-30 seconds, and you don't make such events conscious to your life but sometimes those small memories have the opportunity to convert it into consciousness when we keep a good eye on that. Skills are details, and if you don't pay attention to details, opportunities pass to the next person and whoever grabs its potential, may win.

An alert thinking mind can make us skillful. The idea is to think about when we really need it. We don't lose more by decisions, but by our no decisions. Thinking is not sickness, but thinking unnecessarily makes it sickness. Most people avoid thinking because they find it sad, and by preventing sadness, they prevent reality that could be useful. One should learn to control his thoughts by giving a peaceful end to them. Thoughts don't end until there's an appropriate satisfactory conclusion. So, find the conclusion.

Improving and understanding our skills are extremely slow, even sometimes you can't feel the improvements. When we learn something, we need to make it a part of our life. Thinking about a noble cause is always better than being absent-minded. Occupy your mind with the right thoughts because an idle mind can make us sick of thinking anything. If you have a mind, it will think, and if we don't place what is necessary, something irrelevant will occupy our minds. Remember that.

The world's greatest people aren't extraordinary, but living their life consciously and doing what they think is necessary. People don't disgrace the minimal skills, but the wrong skills. Our consciousness in a subconscious state, makes us unique. Give attention, and you will know what you really love.

Chapter 2

Good and Terrible Mistakes: The Compounding Effect

Do nothing and nothing will change. Do something and everything will get changed.

The difference between an idle person and a highly skillful person is something, small but relevant. If you think you are too small to cause the difference, then you haven't experienced life yet.

Learn from the mistakes of others; that's the statement wandering in our minds when we commit mistakes. Mistakes are underrated because people recognise it as a negative sign of the working process; even the leading industries prevent mistakes when they strike a significant level but we forgot, these companies committed mistakes in their preliminary times with courage. No one accepts mistakes in his work, but you can do it. You want to code an application or a game, learn to swim, review books, collect antiques to acquire a great deal of business, and many more that can sharpen your mind every moment; and in between becoming something, mistakes happen. Learning requires making good mistakes. When we cease making mistakes, we cease learning ahead. Humans understand by doing, not by seeing. If we don't make mistakes, fear will seize us and our capabilities to handle situations will never improve. When we make mistakes while doing something good, it's no longer a mistake, until we make it right. When we see and understand wrong, then we can make it right. The difference is significant. There's a path ahead of good mistakes and if we always get terrified making mistakes, nothing will happen.

Fast learners make mistakes earlier than skillful people. Make good mistakes fast to correct them soon. Even in writing books, the first draft is bullshit, and this happens even in the case of brilliant authors. When we accept mistakes, we encourage our mind to carry out extraordinary things. You may know more and can still make mistakes.

Skills exert a compounding effect. The start is extremely slow, and that's where you have to survive. No one remembers how afraid you are; they remember how much courage you have. Falling from the cliff and jumping from the cliff, both have the difference of fear and courage, respectively.

Chapter 3

The Slow Progress of Skills: Help Yourself

It's good to ask for help, but it's excellent if we try doing it by ourselves.

Helping people is a kind gesture. Getting help is also a magnificent gesture, but in between, we miss a great deal when we knock on other people's doors for small causes. When we talk about skills, we talk about activities that essentially assist us in our everyday work. Developing skills is like making ourselves self-sufficient and confident for the long run. A person can be skillful in many areas, but it requires dedication to get involved in it. Indeed, we can seek help, but repetitive help from people can make us dependent personality. Skills develop slowly in our lives, and they depend on how many problems we try to solve by using our cognitive skills. It's my experience that every time I get a problem, first, I try to solve it by myself, providing I have the potential to do it. The potential to solve a problem, becomes reality when we take actionable efforts. It's the slow progress of skills, but includes exponential progress too. Smart people are an instance of slow progress in skills. We learn when

14

we pay attention to the problems that can be solved and test and utilize our potential to decode them. Also, thinking about a problem requires the proper lone time space and you will be able to recognise your tremendous skills after each day.

Humans develop skills based on the situations they face in life. *The fewer problems they face and solve, the fewer skills they will acquire.* The mind that maintains the attitude to solve problems for any kind of situation, builds skills faster than any other person.

The entire solar energy is extremely dangerous to store, but little by little, the whole world uses that energy in their own way. Mind develops skills when we have good problems and give our best to solve them.

Chapter 4

Fail the Tough Skills: How to Accept Any Tasks!

Humans behave dynamically in diverse environments. They work on how much they know. Are you getting the point? No? Okay, that's not a problem.

Most people work for what they find easy, but we also have a trick that makes your mind to see hard skills as easy ones. Yes, you read it right. Practice the tough skills first and you will also cover the easy ones in a straightforward way. I know you have heard this before, but I want you to accept the logic behind it. Our minds have break-even points for taking risks. If we fail at the tough skills, we can understand, and get succeeded in simple skills of life, but these skills require practice. It's the make-up of the mind to accept toughness, and everything will look easy. ***The more we fear tough skills, the easier skills we ignore.*** Accepting tough tasks pushes our minds for future acceptance.

We know a computer mouse generally has two clicks, left and right. Most people use left as to enter into a program and right click to make small operations but if we interchange the functionality of both clicks, we have to make our mind conscious for the mouse clicks. It's like using implicit memory when nothing is changed, i.e. the functions don't change. When you get conscious, you make the decision and after some time, you will do it automatically. **That's acceptance.**

Fail the skills to strike the back of break-even like Elon Musk.

Chapter 5

Visionary and Exciting Skills: Recognise What Everyone Else is Missing

If we observe people, we will find, most people are working for money; even when people start their career, they consider money as their primary output rather than looking for what interests them. Yes, this is remarkably fascinating to know that most of the rich personalities never looked for money but started with a vision. *These personalities became rich because they were never behind money.* Every work has some vision, and to perceive that, men should be curious and excited at extraordinary levels. We often see extraordinary people mad because they look beyond everyone else. As a result, whenever you have an extraordinary vision, probably, people will laugh at you. Three years back, my mom had learned every skill of cultivating plants from tip to toe on her own. The internet is a boon, if you are really excited about your goals. Every day she learned and applied lessons to grow hundreds of plants, including rare flowers like white & yellow roses and even fruits and vegetables. Growing a plant requires the right level of soil, temperature, water, and consistent care. And the lesson is, nothing can grow in a day. My mom even prepared soil from the waste biodegradable material. If you are aware, ***Delhi is the most polluted city in the world,*** *and growing plants there requires a deep level of caring & even after everything, plants may die.*

When you have a vision, you should equally consider whether the skills will work for your life or not. ***Money is the best and worst motivation and it will work until you earn it. So, for growing skills and motivation, we need something greater than that.*** Money works exponentially for those who don't run behind money. You should have a goal for which you are always stimulated and when you wake up every day, you can gather mind power and accumulate your body strength towards that. Skills don't work in a day because when you are improving, you will face failure, and, in that failure, only faith, curiosity and vision can make you work like hell. Enjoying the skills can make you forget whether you are playing or working hard.

In a **memoir, Newton** wrote, *I don't know what I may appear to the world, but to myself I seem to have been only like a boy playing on the seashore, and diverting myself in now and then finding a smoother pebble or shell than ordinary, whilst the great Ocean of truth lay all undiscovered before me.*

Chapter 6

The Disturbing Elements in Your Work: Control Them Immediately

Humans forget what they don't enforce, and emphasis, but the same can also disturb them deeply if they pierce those thoughts every day. There's no one who is wholly happy in this world. Everyone has stress, problems, sadness, and depression at their own levels. So, assuring others that we suffer with the most complex problems, can make us weak. We all are uncomfortable with something and controlling it with our mindset. *Elon Musk faces more stress than a rational man because it depends on his desire to achieve what he cherishes.* Our level of desires creates stress; that's why someone can be depressed for the things you are genuinely gratified about. Consequently, without desire, you encounter no problems. When you want to work on something, problems occur from every side. Fear weakens our mindset and ability to think great clearly. A completely dedicated mind is required to update skills every day.

First, our own minds can help us to move forward, and the same can stop us from moving ahead. It's not the mind; it's the information we possess in our minds, like what will people think? Am I proficient enough? Will I be capable of achieving this? My friends will abandon me if I don't give enough time to them, my parents will never allow me to follow my interests, how will I survive without money? Everyone is growing and why am I not! Is this relevant to my career and a lot of doubtful questions? Our minds can think frequently even before we speak to one percent. When doubts become more than resolution, we start to doubt everything. A straightforward mind that can think in all directions, can attain skills faster. *Elimination of thoughts isn't possible, but we can control when replacing them with something worthy.* Here are the few significant steps that can assist us protect ourselves from being a disturbing mindset:

A. *Never try reducing a destructive habit, but replace it with a good habit.* Our minds can think constantly about what we want to overlook. So, when we have something good, the mind will regain the good, and the impact of the bad will get reduced. Primarily, it's about stealing the time of when you worry. When you don't have time to worry, the harmful impact will be reduced.

B. *Never ignore the vibes of people.* No one retains the right to make fun of anyone's desire until it's right. People are information for our everyday lives. Get surrounded by the sound people who impart us the energy to achieve our goals. Keep a few close friends or no friends to focus on what you want.

C. *If you have the habit of overthinking, think about your creativity and skills.* Thinking in the appropriate direction creates a moral loop of thinking which can create pleasure to create win-o-win situations for our minds.

D. *The core disturbing element in anyone's work is to expect perfection in their work and accomplishments in very thin time.* Perfection isn't significant, but growth is. When you are learning some skills, never expect results too fast. Skills grow slowly but exponentially.

E. *Are you aware of Murphy's Law? Anything that has the possibility to go wrong, will go wrong, but what we do to make it right, really matters.* When something has the possibility to go bad, consider that and make it right, to move confidently to achieve your goals. Remember, there are bad skills too. Classifying what is good for us, is also a challenging matter to our minds. The human body works on Murphy's Law because if we make no improvements to our body, other things will deteriorate us physically, mentally and emotionally.

Chapter 7

Wander & Wonder: Replicate this!

It's interesting to know that our world was started from imagination, and most of the inventions were done with the help of it. ***The wheel was invented when someone imagined and felt it's need and utility in our lives.*** The question is, why is imagination significant for improving skills? When we acquire skills, we serve people with imagination. It's possible that you are imaging the same as others. ***Everyone has some imagination and wants something that hasn't been created. Therefore, if you can create and solve what people are imagining, you can win in this world.*** Fire was invented when someone felt the need to cook food or someone almost died by shivering. So, the evolution of humans is directly linked to imagination. The whole world is derived by imagination and its absorption, which leads to more imagination to build something that is required.

Imagination is the infinite bricks of walls which are built by human blocks, and no one has ever determined the height of it.

You know, ***Nikola Tesla had an enduring photographic memory where he could memorize everything he had seen.*** You see many people traveling regularly to perceive what's created in the whole world. So, all the work we perceive, represents the art of someone's imagination. Never forget to wander, but remember that; it's the small details that have life; absorb that, and you will get many ideas to upgrade your skills. ***When you wander, wondering is important.*** It's intensely intriguing to give attention to the minute details of life. So, that you can perceive what everyone else is omitting. I travel frequently to make my mind full of valuable ideas, imagination and thoughts.

Indirectly and directly, traveling refreshes our memories, makes us think, engages us in deep details, and helps us to focus on what we really want in life. Better fantastic imagination helps us to think about what can be thinkable. Imagination leads to creativity and ultimately, paying attention to details is the most important attribute anyone can acquire in learning skills.

The mind requires consistent information to get in flow with what we want, and that's why many rich people travel, read and penetrate life with their deep-thinking minds.

Chapter 8

Eliminate, Essential, Execute
Our generation is highly inspired with more execution on tough, but in reality, we need great execution on essentials.

Human lives attract many things and activities because there are a lot of fascinating things that surround us and lure us to accomplish our desires. ***The human mind is a wandering mind. It switches instantly and easily, so we have to decide which life activities are extremely relevant and effective for our lives.*** Sometimes we have the options of two, and none of them is actually bad. Now the confusion arises, and this chapter focuses on choosing the best from the best. Choosing an exceptional skill is good, but choosing the best is still the best option for anyone. Eliminate, Essential, and Execute look connected, but all are different in their definitions. Please examine it carefully to implement them in the right ways.

A. Eliminate: Customarily, most people live till the age of 75 years while some reach the age of around 50, both life ages are good but if we want to get close to what is standard then elimination of a few things are required. You have heard people say, I consume junk food and still feel fit, but the cumulative effect ruins them in the long run. Like a mind that takes stress daily, has more possibility to become depressed one day. Our minds walk on the straight line of easy thoughts and when we enforce something, they will attract. So, ***eliminate what is consuming your productive time or making your time not worthy of being more skilful. Elimination isn't a one-day process, but an everyday process.*** Every day we learn something worthy and terrible too. Finding bad habits and eliminating them before they ruin our schedule is significant. Right now, we can say, never blame the habits when we were actually adopting and enforcing it in our lives.

B. Essential: Look at the kid at the toy store, he wants all the toys from the store irrespective of knowing, he will not be able to play with all. Likewise, humans worship many things in life but can't implement everything as close to perfection. Someday you want to become a cricketer while some days to become an artist. ***Embracing everything doesn't mean we try to achieve everything we love. Division of curiosity bewilders our minds.*** Make a list and understand what you love and then after that choose the most loved activity to focus on.

The highest form of curiosity and dedication bring better results, and they can come out when we follow what we love the most and make our minds work in a single direction.

C. Execute: Recently, Amazon launched the Kindle Vella program in the United States where writers will be rewarded based on episodes read. Most of the leading companies are successful because they research extensively, are swift, and implement to get the first mover advantage. Much love is always given to the invention, and then after, innovations get the less love as compared to it. You have an idea but to know whether it's feasible or not, involvement is significant because in understanding the steps, we forget the hidden human effects, that is invisible and would come out when involvement starts. Building and execution of the skills are immensely important to remain confident and productive. Most people fail because they judge their work only based on how much they know their own sides. How many skills you develop, without usage, they are useless. So, execute skills at regular intervals to know the feasibility of your ideas.

Nothing will improve until we practice, learn, dive deeply, & involve yourself enough to know what to implement and what to leave!

Chapter 9

Hit the Hard-Loved & Tough Skill: Strategy to Reduce Competition

Good among goods is ordinary. Best among the best is extraordinary.

You know, 95% of Youtubers don't get big recognition in the creator section because every second creator is focused on making what the audience enjoys in everyday life. Most creators want views and money, so they get involved in the flow and start making what is trending. That's the harsh reality of the internet. Most skillful creators fail because when they try to do something out of the box, people don't realize it and give decent attention to them. In the internet world, creators are forced to make what people understand and love. In the market, all onions are the same. Some days people start to do what people love, but in reality, the creators don't actually love creating it. If you work on the internet, standing out is significant. *When we serve good among goods, people see it as ordinary because they are already fed-up with seeing such content and skills.* With the internet, people have upgraded, and their sense of understanding has risen so, if you show something good among good, they will leave you like ordinarily, even if you feel best about it.

Also, the remaining 5% creators are the best who have cut the competition with their content. People always look for replacements and substitutes, if you don't replace, the best will remain the best. So, while working confidently and creatively, you can beat 90% of the competition very easily. Hit the hard-loved and tough skills if you genuinely care about being successful, and congratulations, you will become far better than 90% of the people.

Specialization permits you freedom of time, but skills give you freedom of life in the long run.

Chapter 10

Active vs Passive Income: Are Both Significant?

Everyone wants to make money while sleeping, but there's no good sleep without working. Understand, if we offer millions of money to someone who wants to work with dedication and order them to lay down the work, then the money will fail him because humans don't live for money only. So, the people who constantly look for life-time holidays, haven't even observed a week without work because if they have experienced it, they would understand, work is much more significant for humans. Without purpose, active or passive, both incomes are useless until you get the best out of your day and feel an overwhelming sense of accomplishment in your work. Many people think, if they are in place of Elon Musk, they will go on holidays permanently. People say why worry when you have a lot of money. Elon Musk is rich because his goal was never to become rich. He lives on purpose and that's why many people say him the richest poor ever, because he's always been dedicated to working for his companies. Skills development gives us curiosity and satisfaction to believe that we are doing something productive.

A lot of money can't bring satisfaction, but a strong purpose can get you a rich lifestyle because when you work violently to go for money, you will only get money and nothing else. Accordingly, go for satisfaction, whether it's active or passive income.

When love and skill work together, expect a masterpiece. - John Ruskin.

Chapter 11

Introduce New skills: The Loop of Solving Problems

More problems you overlook, the more opportunities you miss. The more problems you solve, the more future problems you avoid.

Skills development isn't a one-day problem solving activity. Every time we try doing something which is greater than our ability, we face problems, and while solving those problems, we can become the person to solve problems of the next level. Most people don't know I manage everything on my own, from idea generation to publishing a book, and in between I encounter many problems. Solving problems is opportunities and every time we solve, we become the person to solve the next bigger problem. People say, I always get a lot of problems in my life and yes, expecting a lot of problems wants you to upgrade to the next level and until you upgrade, the same problems will remain problems. A few years back, I was struggling to make eye-catching good covers. That was a big problem because I was never related to that field. With time and effort, the problem is now my opportunity. Every problem causes a future effect, and if we don't solve it, we will face it again in some next big problem.

Lucky us, we still have people who take care of our earth by contributing in various ways.

The loop of solving problems will never end because the problems have utility of enjoyment and a sense of dedication to solving them. Solving the better problems can help us to resolve the most significant problems in the future. I know, you have heard this many times, but it's the right way to get involved and grow in life.

Most people fail because they expect fewer problems. Expect more problems and solve them with confidence to avoid them in the future.

Chapter 12

Skills Building on Internet: Opportunity But!

The internet is the most fascinating and devastating resource created by humans. As the internet was introduced, spending time on it has increased beyond our expectations. ***No one has ever thought that people will earn money on the internet by making a few clicks.*** The internet makes earning easy as compared to doing a 9 to 5 Job, but someone said it right; everything has both advantages and disadvantages. Earning money on the internet and building skills both are now different. If someone is making too much money on the internet, then that doesn't mean he's skillful, surely. Earning money and building skills are different. If everyone is making money, then it's sure, the quality ways have decreased. Money earning was tough and it's tough today too, but most of the people are only earning money and not even building skills for growth. ***It's much better to ensure you earn money while working on your skills because it will help to get exponential growth in the long run.*** Here are some practical ways to exploit the internet every day and utilize it in the right way:

A. *When you want to use the internet, you should consistently have a purpose* because the internet is full of random information and it will come out every time you use it in a different way. Be specific while using the web and focus on your goals.

B. *Always leave a to-do-list on the table* where you use the internet as every time you try wasting your time, at least it will prompt you to focus.

C. *Remember, the less time you waste on the internet, the more productive time you will have on the internet.* Most people browse the internet, but if you ask what they do, they don't actually know because they randomly get into any stuff provided by the internet.

D. *The internet is a loop of information. Every time you try to peel; a new layer will come.* It's good and bad too. If you are performing productive work, the loop will help you to get better ideas and the opposite can consume your mind entirely.

E. *Sometimes internet skills are a first-mover advantage and that's why people try to get first into every new concept.* Cryptocurrency is the best instance to get the first mover advantage. People who bought a few Bitcoins in 2010, are now billionaires.

F. *Every good is bad sometimes.* Build skills on the internet but get a real interactive outside environment to refresh your mindset every day.

Chapter 13

What Hinders Our Skills Development: The Fear Factor Barrier

Our minds have the capacity to solve any problem, if it works, and gets utilized effectively, but most ideas fail because most people have the fear of getting failed. I know, it's the most common line you have ever heard. What's so cool about being not afraid. Most people have declared it decades back, but I can assure you, this is still the most common problem in any country. Fear isn't a psychological problem but a conclusion-based problem. Humans have the habit of expecting tremendous results before working on something. Expecting good results never allows people to work with bad results. What if I fail; the thought comes, and most of the ideas fail in their minds. Executing skills is much more significant than building thousands of skills in your mind.

Learn, build, adapt, alter, implement, alter again, implement, and alter again until it becomes your best.

Knowledge is useless until it is applied.

Chapter 14

The Significance of Dissatisfaction

Do you ever feel that most billionaires are dissatisfied even when they can live their lives without worrying for thousands of years? Why is Elon Musk so interested in going to Mars? Yeah, I know the world is really creepy where a few are struggling for food and a few are going to Mars. Humans are dissatisfied with what they have and this dissatisfaction can make some people think about why people think out of the box when there's no box. I know there's a lot of confusion because a few minutes back, I told you to get satisfied with your work, understand, always get satisfied with what you accomplished but dissatisfied for something new, while not disturbing and stressing your life. It's not about complete dissatisfaction but partial satisfaction.

Warren Buffett reads a lot of books in a day, and he gets satisfied with the knowledge he has acquired and works for more. Urging for more is important if you undoubtedly want to forget who is at number one.

When you get dissatisfied with your work, then you discover what satisfies your work. The dissatisfaction arises to get more satisfaction and confidence in your skills.

Chapter 15

The Impossibility of Skills: Tough Skills in Life

Everything is impossible until someone finds the solution and makes it possible.

Adaptation is the king of this era. If you can adapt, you can create. Sometimes we feel the world is at exponential growth where soon, we will expect extremely impossible ideas in the future. I recommend you to go for impossible tough skills than to go for something that has already been accepted because people's break-even point to get astonishment has increased. Now, electric cars are no wonder for people who don't even have cars, and that is why people are dissatisfied. If you think you have the idea to create something exceptional, then you should create it. Recently, a man had developed a small version of a jeep from scrap spare parts in a few years, and when **Industrialist Anand Mahindra** recognized it from Twitter, he offered him a brand-new Bolero in exchange for it. The company also promised him that his car would be displayed in **Mahindra**

Research Valley, but he denied by saying, he created the car because he doesn't have money to buy a car and manage it, even if I take the Bolero, I will not manage it well. My family is entirely dependent on this small car, and my whole business depends on it. You know, the man had created the car because he essentially needed it. His family also wanted to travel in a car but couldn't be able to afford it. Everything is possible when you are in need and love.

Like him, we heard about the news of tremendous innovations that seem impossible, but some people's hard work and will make it possible. When we have need, we can achieve anything well.

You know, *Isaac Newton died alone, and broke*, but he was deeply indulged in his work. He had no hobbies and never married; and when we look closely at his life, we find, he had actually no time to waste. Newton usually worked from 10 am to 6 pm continuously and went for dinner at the same restaurant and after that, worked till 3 am. He never slept more than 3 hours and sometimes he even worked on his research for 3 or 4 days continuously.

Everyone has different kinds of goals; and their goals matter to them only and may feel useless to others. It's your life to recognize what is important to you. If you want to work deeply, work for it, everything else matters after that. And remember, never work to impress because it may not last longer.

Chapter 16

The Everyday Routine in Building Skills: Vital Rules for Implementation.

Balance the good and bad in your minds; instead of focusing on only good or only bad - both situations are harmful to the minds.

Neither every day will be favourable to your mind nor every day your mind will support your body, but every day it's more than that. Developing an admirable skill requires madness and an unshakeable will. Some people leave the growth of skills when they start earning enough money for their livelihood and a great standard of living. A considerable skill isn't always required for money but to maintain an enthusiasm and energetic vibe in our lives. Most people feel bored in life because they only focus on earning money and after that their work environment becomes monotonous. Plus, when you feel negative, you should feel optimistic or do something that imparts the sense of love to you. Everyday routine may feel good if you have curiosity about growth or some life achievement.

Implement these rules in your everyday life to see your life growing and be happily living:

A. Go for natural skills for which you are curious mostly and feel energetic around them.

B. Stay away from negative people who question your skills every time, even in the way of jokes. Everything has an impact, whether we believe it or not.

C. When you learn something, accept the things you know and don't know, to know the real status of your productivity. If you always feel like you know everything, productivity may stop.

D. Before, during and after working, feel calm about what you have concluded; instead of worrying about what you could have done. Change the way you look at your work and stay ready for the next day.

E. Wasting today is also like consuming energy for tomorrow. If you work happily today, maybe tomorrow, you will work better than before.

F. Upgrading everything is good, but it's useless if we always look for tomorrow. Work for today and enjoy today because tomorrow we have nothing created, even if we know nothing about it.

G. Maintain personal life balance and never ignore the power of love. Not every day you win, but if you have someone good on your side, you will succeed later.

H. Listen to people even if you are the only intelligent person in the world because listening modifies the words we assume right. We should listen to others as well.

I. Solve even the tiny problems you face in everyday life because avoidance of problems creates more problems in life. Problems create genius.

J. Multitasking is a big myth and confusion to our minds. Our minds need healing and energy. It doesn't need the stuffing, but the believing. When you do one work at a time, concentration and dedication improve.

K. Be like a slow tortoise. Don't rush to accomplish everything in a day or week. Be curious, questionable & never leave what you want to understand. In fact, there's no existence of a slow tortoise. When we hear about the tortoise, slowness is implied and that's his power.

The greatest enemy of knowledge is not ignorance. It's the illusion of knowledge. - Stephen King.

Chapter 17

Complex Problems, Tough Procedure, & Simple Outcome: The Stages in Skill Development!

Creating what customers want and in a straightforward way, can build the most successful business in any century. When a customer seeks a product, he doesn't expect any kind of trouble; in fact, he wants ease even in case of complex products. When a business produces any kind of goods or services, it undergoes an end number of tough procedures, so that the customers don't have to go through it. It's like thinking like customers for customers and reducing what they could expect negatively. Even if a customer purchases a product which needs to be assembled, the company provides every single assistance that can make procedure easy. Decathlon, the number one sports brand, makes Domyos exercise cycle where customers have to assemble the product on their own and the company provides everything just for one time assemble and even the basic tools, so that customers don't feel irritated while doing it.

Anything we consume in our daily life, even a single sachet, goes through many vicious procedures. For a simple result, complex problems need to be solved while considering every circumstance. If you want to design a clean website, you need to go through every complex problem and tough procedure; and ultimately, we call them the stages of skill development.

Businessmen don't think simply; they think deeply, practically, emotionally and problematically because every problem they miss, the customers will get hurt. So, facing complex problems isn't problems but the process to make everything simple to impart services easily and remember when you provide goods and services to customers, simplicity takes all the credit. No one wants to face complexity in everyday life.

The results of skills training are usually easy, but behind the curtain, the process is complicated. *Every skill has buyers and sellers, but your skill decides its exposure.*

Chapter 18

One Day; One Task: The Mind Hack

Multitasking is very popular these days and most people accept it to produce fast results. I also admire multitasking, but we should understand what it actually is because when we do the work, we don't pay attention to it. When I talk about attention, I talk about mind attention, an absolute dedication to achieving the best results. ***Concentration, dedication and attention are important elements to solving a problem.*** While doing something else and paying partial attention, can bring partial results. To solve a problem, you have to live it. Living doesn't require multitasking, but concentration. ***To live peacefully, someone should get dedicated to the purpose and get attached passionately.*** We recommend you to do one task in a day and decide what to do for the whole day, so your mind doesn't get puzzled and you can work peacefully throughout the entire day. With confusion, the mind doesn't accomplish things properly. Multitasking isn't bad, but it reduces productivity to think clearly and properly.

Multitasking helps you to complete tasks but reduces your mind's capacity to settle one's thoughts deeply, which actually helps you to solve problems. Always remember, you don't only have to complete the tasks but achieve the tasks in your mind too, because it's useless if your mind feels thirsty for satisfaction and you achieved the tasks somehow. Your mind should feel satisfied and that can feel when you get attached to the purpose deeply.

To absorb skills for a long time, one should do one work at a time to get lost in it. Remember that.

<h1 style="text-align:center">Chapter 19</h1>

Brainstorming Skills: Never Get Bored With Them!

Do you ever feel that sometimes your mind works fast and develops thoughts swiftly, while some days it works slow? Affirmative, it's possible that some days we feel active and our minds bring out great ideas, while some days, like we feel blank inside our mind and nothing works out. Humans experience this because the mind is a machine, and the less we utilize it, the more time it would take to get restored to the normal state to think great. So, to keep getting better and active ideas, we need to keep our minds active to absorb what most people neglect. It's the brilliant power of the human mind. Like, when we travel, we feel energetic and start to absorb and perceive even the little details. It happens because at that time, our minds get active and open to the environment and we create photographic memories too. To keep our minds active, we need doing the things we love in our everyday life or maybe in some cases, we need to develop habits so our minds take interest, absorb and help us to solve problems.

As a writer, I always love reading a lot of articles every day. I read books and listen to music to keep my mind active in any environment. *The more bored you feel, the less creative you will be. Working isn't important, but working actively is important.* Such cognitive development activities keep our minds active in interacting with the environment and help us to absorb novel ideas and skills.

Even death has a goal to find another life & what are you doing with your life! Don't ignore insignificant skills because skills are a sum of solved problems.

Chapter 20

The Core of Discipline: The Master Key

The most common mistake people make in the 21st century is to expect fast success with no failure.

As life goes long, the man should have a purpose that can go on long without loss of any enthusiasm in between. Whatever goal we choose, it has an end and that sometimes leads to a loss of energy in life later. Our goals aren't always to accomplish but to enjoy the process for the whole life. Like, most people study to become successful, to lead a great life, it's good, but losing what makes us move, is like losing our purpose after we achieve. After winning, most people leave their work as what they wanted, in their hands, then. People lose discipline in their work when they get what they want and ultimately their life becomes monotonous. *Discipline directs us to do what we always love for our whole life, even if we have accomplished our goals.* The vital role in building skills in discipline is to continue even after winning. Until winning, people have high energy and after that they become gloomy. Having everything isn't the goal, but discipline is.

Humans hurry to accomplish what they want for their whole life. A happy life and a disciplined mind always keep work going even after he wins because that's where you will have the both success and mind accomplishment.

Humans without purpose and discipline make their journey difficult to live life till death.

Chapter 21

Make Subconscious Skills Conscious: Repeat the Mind Exercise.

Thinking more than you need is evil. Thinking less than you need is escaping, and thinking right is the summation of conscious and subconscious mind understanding.

The same person with the same resources can be happy or sad. It's irrelevant to see mind discipline and stability only with people's external happiness and how they behave. Humans bury a lot of information and secrets in their minds subconsciously, and that information supports or disturbs them most of the time. It's useless to say our minds stop thinking because it's the function, but what we think, can be changed. When we think consciously, our subconscious mind supports us silently and makes us think about what is dominating in our subconscious mind. Basically, our subconscious mind gives reasons and connects the dots for what our conscious mind wants to think and accept. Most minds are stuck in that loop because they think consciously only and don't understand the subconscious mind. Understand, I said if you do something bad to someone, you make your conscious mind satisfied by giving various statements, but inside our subconscious mind never accept the wrong fact. That's why it's difficult to control our subconscious mind because we can't deny the truth; and most of the people who do something wrong, remain unhappy somewhere.

Now, can we control both the conscious and subconscious mind? It could be possible. Most people avoid information in the 21st century and think they will be happy after that, and it's possible but main problem isn't the information but the wrong information; and in fact, most information in our generation is wrong and that information enters our subconscious mind to think consciously like that. My purpose for the explanation is simple. *We have a lot of good habits that work silently but are actually good. We have to keep those habits conscious to bring that into our everyday lives. The chief idea of reading a book works for our conscious mind.* When we read books, a lot of information goes into our subconscious mind but remains locked until we make it conscious and make it useful.

Humans carry a lot of ideas, information, good and bad habits in their subconscious minds. What our conscious mind thinks, the subconscious mind sends us that kind of information, and also, our subconscious mind forms the conscious mind, so they are entirely dependent on each other. Your skills aren't only dependent on your conscious mind, but on what you aren't even thinking, though.

The Good and Guilt remain with humans throughout life. We can't escape, but can control only.

Chapter 22

The Gist of Exercising & Implementation of Rules

Books aren't for reading only. They are for experimentation and absorption. We recommend every reader to make a diary to note down what they learn every day. Make your notes, to not waste what you read today. Here are the quick lessons that can make you think and be skillful throughout your whole life:

A. Humans develop skills based on situations available to them. The less problems they face, the less skills they will acquire. The minds which have the attitude to solve problems in any situation, build skills faster than any other.

B. Accept what you already know. Understand your potential and learn what will work best for you.

C. We should learn skills when we are calm, minded, and focused, to allow the satisfaction of work in our minds too. We should control what will go on in our minds. Most people don't think because they think their own mind fights between right and wrong.

D. It's better to make mistakes to make them good by learning and understanding. Mistakes can be good or bad, but the worst is the fear that stops us from making mistakes. Mistakes are necessary to understand what will work because we all do something uniquely for the first time.

E. Highly skillful people have the fate to be alone and learn. We should understand what they are actually doing. Great people see and observe everything. They bring out what is significant to them.

F. It's not about what skills you want. You can learn and achieve any skills, but understand; procedure is the same and sometimes long enough to reach the right place.

G. Without loving someone, maybe your world will be silent; but without loving our life aim, our life will be miserable.

H. Skills sharpen knowledge. Knowledge is the dormant mind, useless like a great book in the museum.

I. Skills filter the right knowledge & that brings smooth execution.

J. Humans can't be busy for long in the work they don't even love, but if they love something, they will be lost forever and their life will be happy and peaceful.

K. Complicated the process - simple the results in Business.

L. Everyone has life problems, but one should have the skills to ignore them and work best in life.

M. Knowledge is not skill, knowledge plus ten thousand times is skill. - Shinichi Suzuki.

N. Usually, the key to success and learning aren't the genius mind but the curious and disciplined mind to learn quickly.

O. The Great attributes to acquire the most valuable skills in the World: Interest, curiosity, habit to sit alone, praising yourself, learning to fail, habits to fail, get irritated & still get back to work, no early money, a lot of time (may be less), sacrificing few activities, dedication, determination, learning and applying, looking for scope for improvement, ready to get hate or no appreciation, and most significant, thinking straight and clear.

P. He who can take no interest in what is small, will take false interest in what is great; he who cannot make a bank sublime, will make a mountain ridiculous. - John Ruskin.

About the Author

DEEPAK GUPTA is pre-eminently known for writing plain sailing, meticulous, and pragmatic Self-Help books. He's the author of **more than forty books** including **10 Principles to Beat Failure** that won **Google Best Choice 2018** & became **Top Seller on Google Play Store in 2019**. He has been garnering much acclaim for his **30 Minutes Read & 10 Principles Series**. Till now, he has received **500k+ readership** & **a lot of appreciation** from all over the world. He believes in writing & living best exceptional content from his subconscious mind. He loves to observe, absorb, and write on various social issues, inspirational truthful words, short stories, and heart whelming poetry. Also, he has travelled to many places in India like Manali, Rajasthan, Goa, Kolkata, Madhya Pradesh, Jammu, Dalhousie, and Mussoorie to bring originality in his work. He *releases new short books every month* to get readers to connect with the truth of life.

Deepak Gupta received his post-graduation degree from **Delhi School of Economics**. Also, when he's not writing, he can be found wandering on his **exquisite terrace garden**. He lives with his family in **Delhi, India**.

Keep in touch with Deepak via the web:
Instagram @authordeepakgupta
Facebook: facebook.com/authordeepakgupta
Twitter @authordeepakgup

Don't miss out!

Visit the website below and you can sign up to receive emails whenever Deepak Gupta publishes a new book. There's no charge and no obligation.

https://books2read.com/r/B-A-AQXE-JUJVB

BOOKS 2 READ

Connecting independent readers to independent writers.

Did you love *The Rules of Being Highly Skillful*? Then you should read *10 Principles To Beat Failure: Illustrated Enhanced Edition*[1] by Deepak Gupta!

Implement drop in the ocean of knowledge and you can make ocean out of the drop.

Life is not as plain-sailing as we think. It has the habit to create hurdles in our path. Whenever we try to do something great, people will come and laugh at us. This is the universal law. 10 Principles to Beat Failure can help you with the following Concepts & Problems:

How to be Happy Consistently.Problems related Truths &

---

1. https://books2read.com/u/m0gvyY

2. https://books2read.com/u/m0gvyY

Myths.How to execute plans.How to feel satisfied at the end of day.How to set your Goals Strongly.How to say NO to unwanted tasks.How to understand Rights & Wrongs to Success.Why we fail at execution of Goals.Do's & Don'ts in Morning Schedule.How to understand your Satisfaction Level.How to be Successful Consistently.How to build Bullet-Proof Success.How to Celebrate Success.How to Increase Knowledge.The Attributes of Visionary People.How to Free your Mind.The Classical Conditioning of Life.How to Work in Panic.How to Link Appreciation with Results.How to attract more people to our products.How to not be a Rat.The Bandersnatch to take Best Life Decisions.How to get more ideas everyday.The Game of Mindset.How to decide our Mind Feed.

What to expect in NEW ILLUSTRATED ENHANCED EDITION 2021:

★ **Added 32 New Chapters, Bonuses, and Illustrations which will help readers to understand Success and Failure Principles in much Simplified Manner.**

★ **Revised All Principles with Best Possible Practical Practices.**

Every day is the day to get up again and to learn something innovative and creative. To become a superior person, we should learn to observe our nature and understand the latent power inside it. Our power lies in to understand the invincible love and greatest power of our mind. But how much we focus to create our mind happy and healthy? Have we ever thought of this matter? How many negative thoughts have unconsciously latent in our mind? How we waste our energy every day because of our purposeless negative thoughts. We never focus on the depth of our mind as we always busy in our run and races &

money and faces. Being good is not only a matter of the good heart but also the matter of the beautiful mind to cope up with the end number of life failures. If you want to become cheery and to take the right decision, then you should understand the beautiful nerves of your mind.

10 Principles To Beat Failure includes ten mind boggling principles that will change your life forever and boost you to achieve your dreams and aspirations at any stage of life.

We have to ask questions, not because we want to know the answers. Answers don't exist universally. They exist in the form to make fit in our life. What make us satisfied is our answers.

Read more at https://www.authordeepakgupta.com.

Also by Deepak Gupta

15 Minutes Read
Common Sense in the 21st Century

30 Minutes Read
How To Deal With Haters
One Second Rule: How to take Right Decisions quickly without Thinking too Much
Hard Decisions Easy Life: Bandersnatch & The World of Possibilities
Sell Your Talent: How to Convert Talent into Money along with the Personality Development
Ideas & Origami
The Anti-Suicidal Self Help Book
The Therapy of Peace: Illustrated Edition
The Rules of Being Highly Productive
How to Think Everyday
Bedtime Thinker
The Rules of Being Highly Skillful
Blockchain Technology: The Future

Power
The Power of Universe
The Power of Nothing: They say and We do

Year of Short Stories
But She Didn't Come

Standalone
Inspiring Life
Zero Degree: An Icy Thriller
She: She Heals Everything
10 Principles To Beat Failure: Illustrated Enhanced Edition
Beta 2020
10 Principles To Love Yourself
How To Heal Yourself
She: She heals everything
Skyfall: Your Heart Will Fall Too
The Girl With No Dreams
The Pigeon With Broken Legs: Modern Classics Children
Story
Average Mind: The World is not the Wonder. It's the Wonder
which makes your World
Being Busy Is Not Always Productive: Stop Wasting your Time
at the Wrong Place

Happiness Without Cause: Why Happiness was easy in the 19th Century but not in the 21st Century

Alone Than Lonely: How to Live Life without Attachment & Enjoy your Company

The Lost Child

The Power Pack of Short Stories: Box Set of Crime, Thriller & Suspense Stories

Earth 2200

Amazon Kindle & Google Play ebooks Pricing System: Maximize Your ebooks Sales

5 Principles To Dig Out Success

????: Udhaar

The Little Book of Wise Quotes

Deepak Gupta Collection: The Complete Self Help Book (2015-2020)

Revenge

Revolutionary Love: Friendship-Love-Revenge: A Novel

The Man Who Forgets

Watch for more at https://www.authordeepakgupta.com.

www.ingramcontent.com/pod-product-compliance
Lightning Source LLC
Chambersburg PA
CBHW031223160726
47992CB00006B/2871